For my children—
Dirk, Alivia, and Brooks
and in memory of Robert

Follow and Do

The Lord's Supper

Written and Illustrated by Joni Walker

CONCORDIA PUBLISHING HOUSE · SAINT LOUIS

Dear Parents,

"Come Lord Jesus. ..." "Come, oh come, Emmanuel. ..."
"Thy kingdom come. ..." We pray often that Christ comes to us.
In the Lord's Supper, through His called and ordained servant,
He does just that.

The Jesus who comes to us in **Holy Communion** is not the ethereal
Jesus, the feelings-in-the-heart kind of Jesus. It is not a symbolic
Christ. This Jesus places His real self in the **bread and wine**—
real presence—for us. This is God in the reality of His Word and the
tangible elements providing us with forgiveness, renewal, and strength.

In our **traditions**, young children do not receive the Lord's Supper,
but they often have questions about it, finding it a mysterious and
curious ritual.

Even little ones can learn about the special reality that Jesus still
does very real things for us. Many congregations invite children to

come to the altar with their parents. This allows the *youngest* members an up-close look at the Sacrament and teaches them the ritual long before they participate in it. In this way, parents and church alike teach children about the *divine service*, fulfilling an important vow made at the child's Baptism, that we "provide for his further instruction in the Christian faith, his baptismal grace and in communion with the Church."

Our Savior invites us to His table regardless of our state. We come to the altar as sinful people. We leave wrapped in His grace and filled with the PEACE that comes only from knowing His mercy and from being certain of His promises.

We don't know when Jesus will come again in the flesh or when He will call us to be with Him. Nevertheless, until then He comes to be with us in this very real way. "COME, LORD JESUS..." and He does!

What is the Sacrament of the Altar?

It is the true body and blood of our Lord Jesus Christ under the bread and wine, instituted by Christ Himself for us Christians to eat and to drink.

Where is this written?

The holy Evangelists Matthew, Mark, Luke, and St. Paul write:

Our Lord Jesus Christ, on the night when He was betrayed, took bread, and when He had given thanks…

He broke it and gave it to the disciples and said: "Take, eat; this is My body, which is given for you. This do in remembrance of Me."

In the same way also He took the cup after supper, and when He had given thanks,

He gave it to them, saying,

"Drink of it, all of you; this cup is the new testament in My blood, which is shed for you for the forgiveness of sins. This do, as often as you drink it, in remembrance of Me."

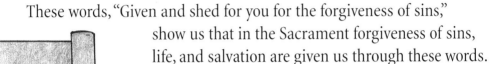

What is the benefit of this eating and drinking?

These words, "Given and shed for you for the forgiveness of sins," show us that in the Sacrament forgiveness of sins, life, and salvation are given us through these words. For where there is forgiveness of sins, there is also life and salvation.

How can bodily eating and drinking do such great things?

Certainly not just eating and drinking do these things, but the words written here: "Given and shed for you for the forgiveness of sins."

These words, along with the bodily eating and drinking, are the main thing in the Sacrament. Whoever believes these words has exactly what they say: "forgiveness of sins."

Who receives this sacrament worthily?

Fasting and bodily preparation are certainly fine outward training.

But that person is truly worthy and well prepared who has faith in these words: "Given and shed for you for the forgiveness of sins."

But anyone who does not believe these words or doubts them is unworthy and unprepared, for the words **"for you"** require all hearts to believe.

Published by Concordia Publishing House
3558 S. Jefferson Avenue, St. Louis, MO 63118-3968
1-800-325-3040 • www.cph.org

Manufactured in China

1 2 3 4 5 6 7 8 9 10   14 13 12 11 10 09 08 07 06 05